PIANO / VOCAL / GUITAR

NEEDTOBREATHE

SHEET MUSIC COLLECTION

ISBN 978-1-70515-311-6

Visit Hal Leonard Online at
www.halleonard.com

World headquarters, contact:
Hal Leonard
7777 West Bluemound Road
Milwaukee, WI 53213
Email: info@halleonard.com

In Europe, contact:
Hal Leonard Europe Limited
42 Wigmore Street
Marylebone, London, W1U 2RN
Email: info@halleonardeurope.com

In Australia, contact:
Hal Leonard Australia Pty. Ltd.
4 Lentara Court
Cheltenham, Victoria, 3192 Australia
Email: info@halleonard.com.au

BANKS

Words and Music by NATHANIEL RINEHART,
WILLIAM RINEHART and TRENT DABBS

BROTHER

Words and Music by NATHANIEL RINEHART,
GAVIN DeGRAW and WILLIAM RINEHART

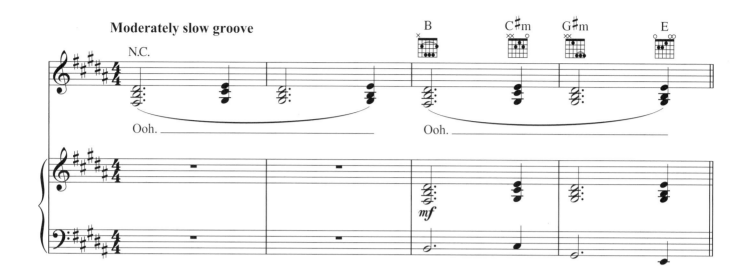

Moderately slow groove

Ooh. _____ Ooh. _____

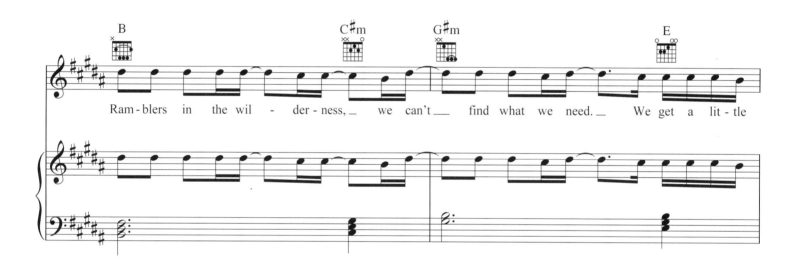

Ram-blers in the wil-der-ness, _ we can't _ find what we need. _ We get a lit-tle

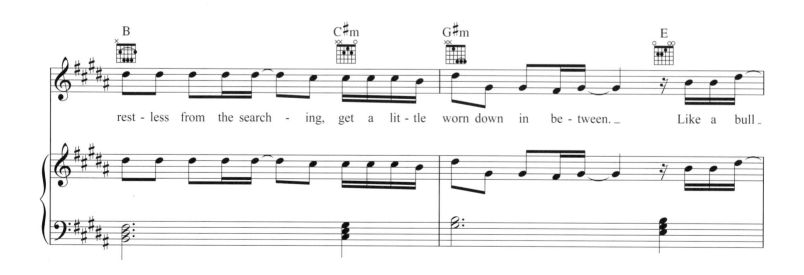

rest-less from the search-ing, get a lit-tle worn down in be-tween. _ Like a bull _

FOREVER ON YOUR SIDE

Words and Music by NATHANIEL RINEHART
and WILLIAM RINEHART

Moderately

I won't pre-tend

that we can __ con-trol the night or what kind __ of

road we're on, _____ or where we __ will see the light.

HAPPINESS

Words and Music by NATHANIEL RINEHART,
WILLIAM RINEHART, WHITNEY PHILLIPS
and IDO ZMISHLANY

Moderate Rock beat

Sing - ing, oh, _____ hap - pi - ness. _____ Sing - ing,

oh, _____ hap - pi - ness. _____ I got a

home - sick heart, but a long ways left to go. _____ I've been

HARD LOVE

Words and Music by NATHANIEL RINEHART
and WILLIAM RINEHART

(Oh, _____ oh.) _____

Male: Trad-ing punch-es with the heart of dark - ness; goin' to blows with your fear in-car - nate.

Nev-er gone un-til it's stripped a - way; but part of you has got-ta die to change. _

KEEP YOUR EYES OPEN

Words and Music by NATHANIEL RINEHART
and WILLIAM RINEHART

Moderate Rock beat

If you could sol - dier on, ____ head - strong in - to the storm, ____
Just past the cir - cum - stance, ____ the first light, a sec - ond chance. ____

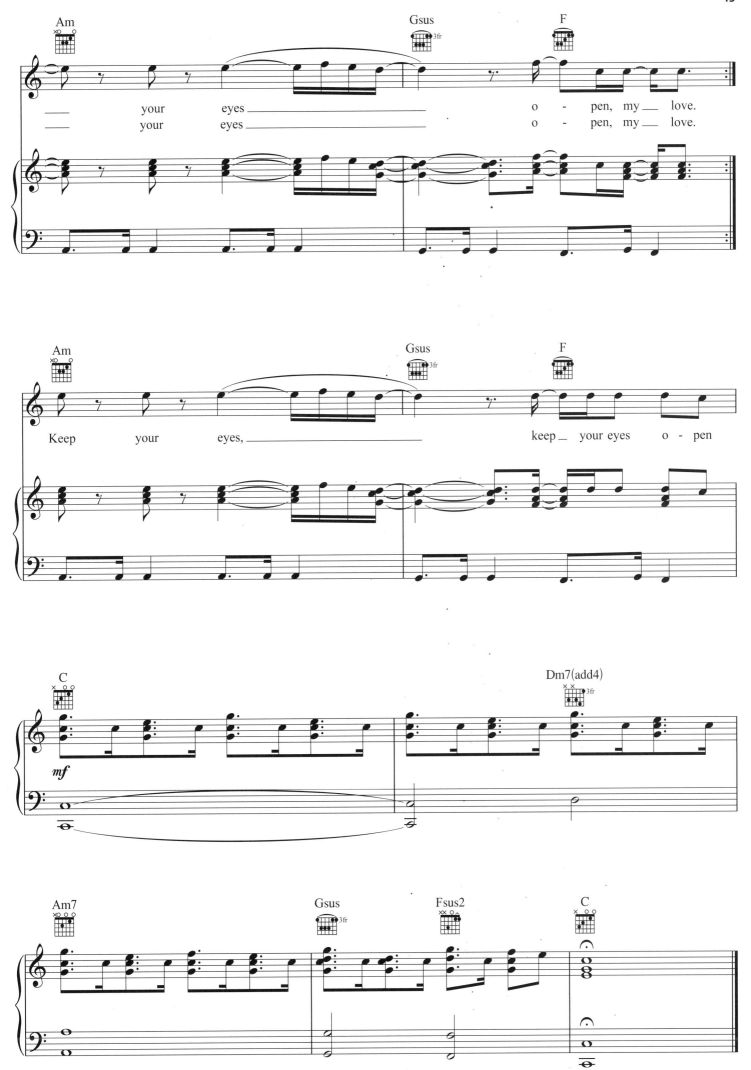

I AM YOURS

Words and Music by
WILLIAM RINEHART

I WANNA REMEMBER

Words and Music by WILLIAM RINEHART,
JORDAN REYNOLDS and PARKER WELLING

Moderate Acoustic Rock

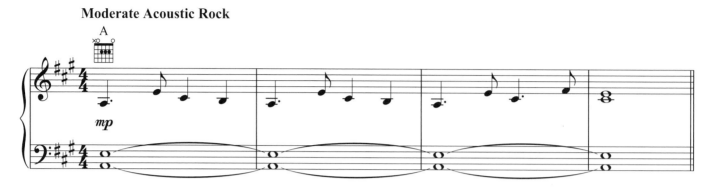

Male: This feels like one of those mo - ments mov - ing by so fast, you
Breathe it in, the feel of your bod - y on my fin - ger - tips, the

wan - na do some - thing just to make it last. You wan - na do some - thing to re - mem -
moon - light on fi - re and the clothes we're in. We got - ta do some - thing to re - mem -

INTO THE MYSTERY

Words and Music by
WILLIAM RINEHART

Moderate Acoustic Rock

It's hard to see ___ it, ___ still be-lieve it. ___

You have al - ways ___ lived deep in - side ___ my heart. ___

LET'S STAY HOME TONIGHT

Words and Music by NATHANIEL RINEHART,
WILLIAM RINEHART and LUKE LAIRD

Half-time feel

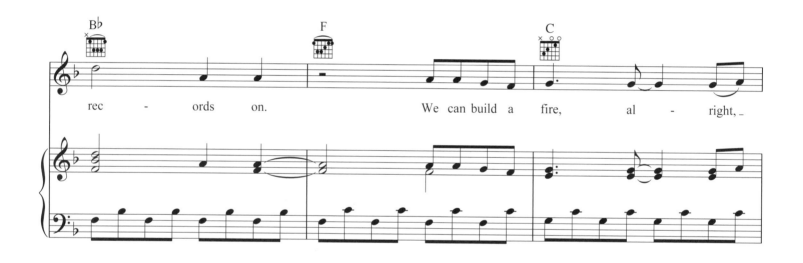

MULTIPLIED

Words and Music by NATHANIEL RINEHART
and WILLIAM RINEHART

Folk Rock feel

Your love is ____

like ra - di - ant dia - monds _____ burst - ing ___ in -

side us, ___ we can - not _____ con - tain.

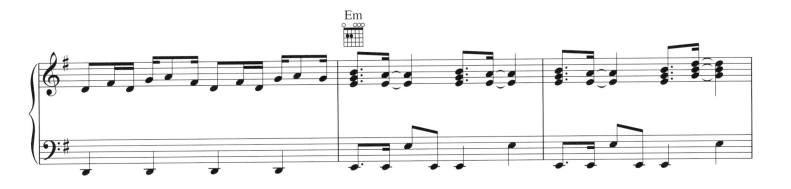

Your

skies, _____ and these hal - le - lu - jahs _ be mul - ti -

plied.

(Vocal ad lib. on repeat)

SEASONS

Words and Music by NATHANIEL RINEHART,
JOSH LOVELACE, SETH BOLT
and WILLIAM RINEHART

Moderately fast

We can't de-cide if we are fall-

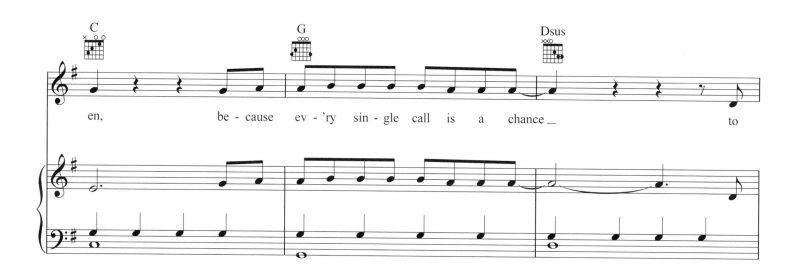

en, be-cause ev-'ry sin-gle call is a chance ___ to

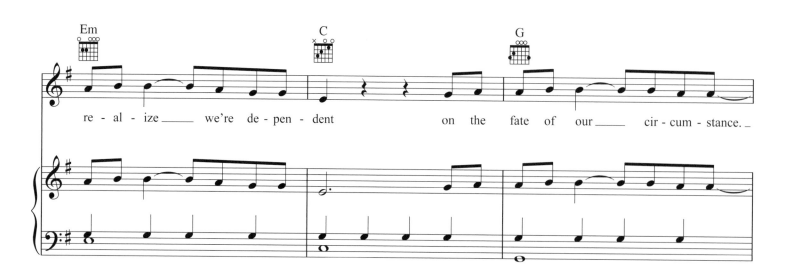

re-al-ize ___ we're de-pen-dent on the fate of our ___ cir-cum-stance. ___

SOMETHING BEAUTIFUL

Words and Music by NATHANIEL RINEHART
and WILLIAM RINEHART

Moderate Rock

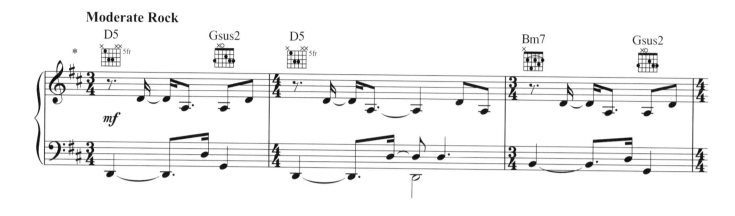

In your o - cean,_ I'm an - kle deep. I feel the

waves crash - in' on my _____ feet. It's like I know where _ I need to

* Recorded a half step lower.

TESTIFY

Words and Music by NATHANIEL RINEHART
and WILLIAM RINEHART

Acoustic Folk Rock

Give me your heart, give me your song, sing it with all your might.

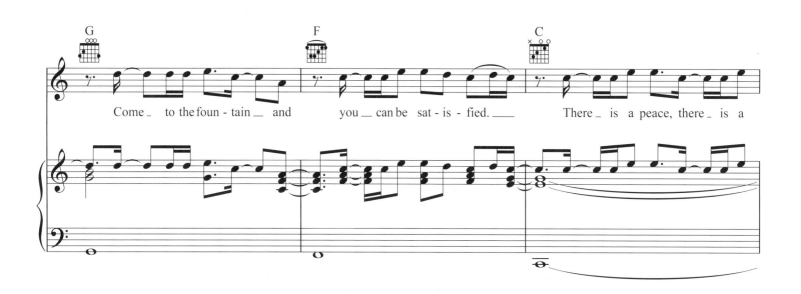

Come to the foun-tain and you can be sat-is-fied. There is a peace, there is a

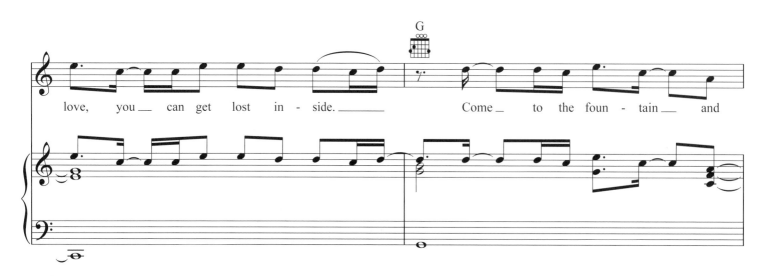

love, you can get lost in-side. Come to the foun-tain and

WASHED BY THE WATER

Words and Music by NATHANIEL RINEHART
and WILLIAM RINEHART

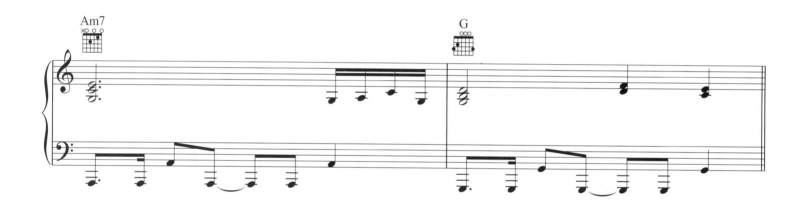

Dad-dy was a preach-er, she was____ his wife,____

* *Recorded a half step lower.*

WHO AM I

Words and Music by WILLIAM RINEHART,
CASON COOLEY, JORDAN REYNOLDS,
THOMAS RHETT and JEREMY LUTITO